J Bayview

D0759211

NORTH AMERICA

Go Exploring! Continents and Oceans

By Steffi Cavell-Clarke

©This edition was published in 2018. First published in 2017.

Book Life
King's Lynn
Norfolk PE30 4LS

ISBN: 978-1-78637-045-7

Written by:
Steffi Cavell-Clarke

Edited by:
Grace Jones

Designed by:
Natalie Carr

A catalogue record for this book is available from the British Library.

All facts, statistics, web addresses and URLs in this book were verified as valid and accurate at time of writing. No responsibility for any changes to external websites or references can be accepted by either the author or publisher.

NORTH AMERICA

CONTENTS

Words in **red** can be found in the glossary on page 23.

WHAT IS A CONTINENT?

A continent is a very large area of land that covers part of the Earth's surface. There are seven continents in total. There are also five oceans that surround the seven continents.

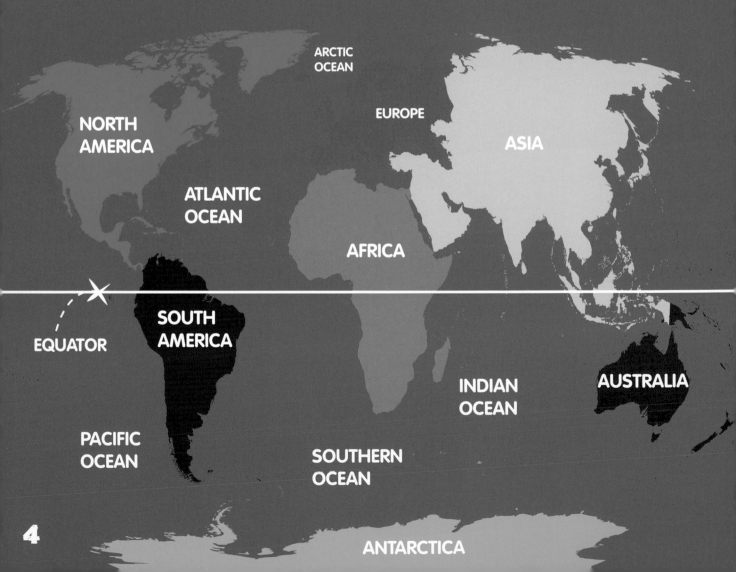

ARCTIC OCEAN

EUROPE

ASIA

NORTH AMERICA

ATLANTIC OCEAN

AFRICA

SOUTH AMERICA

EQUATOR

INDIAN OCEAN

AUSTRALIA

PACIFIC OCEAN

SOUTHERN OCEAN

ANTARCTICA

The seven continents are home to the Earth's **population.** Each continent has many different types of weather, landscape and wildlife. Let's go exploring!

WHERE IS NORTH AMERICA?

North America is **located** to the north of South America and to the west of Europe. It is almost completely surrounded by ocean. The Pacific Ocean is to the west, the Atlantic Ocean to the east and the Arctic Ocean is to the north of North America.

Canyonlands in North America

North America

South America

The continent of North America includes many islands. These are areas of land that are completely surrounded by water. Greenland is the biggest island in North America.

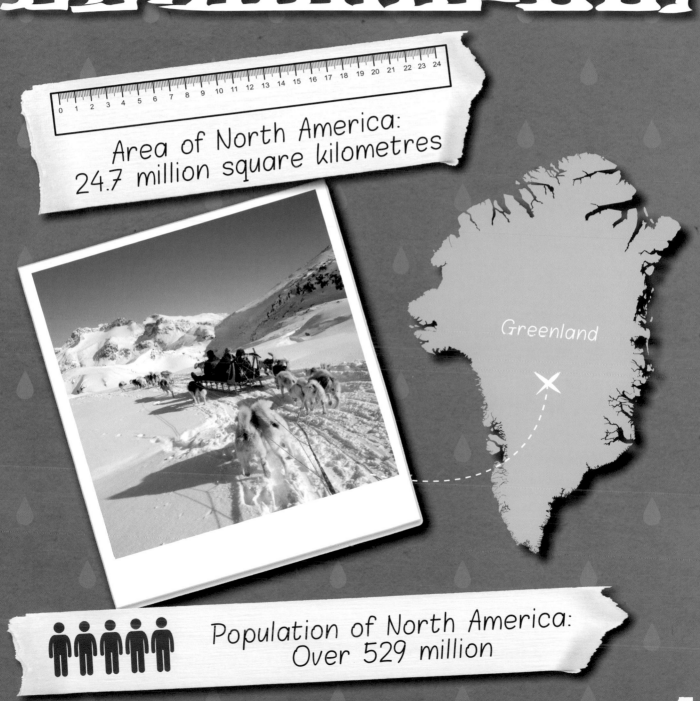

Area of North America:
24.7 million square kilometres

Greenland

Population of North America:
Over 529 million

OCEANS

A sea is an extremely large area of saltwater. The biggest seas in the world are called oceans. Just like countries, seas and oceans have different names.

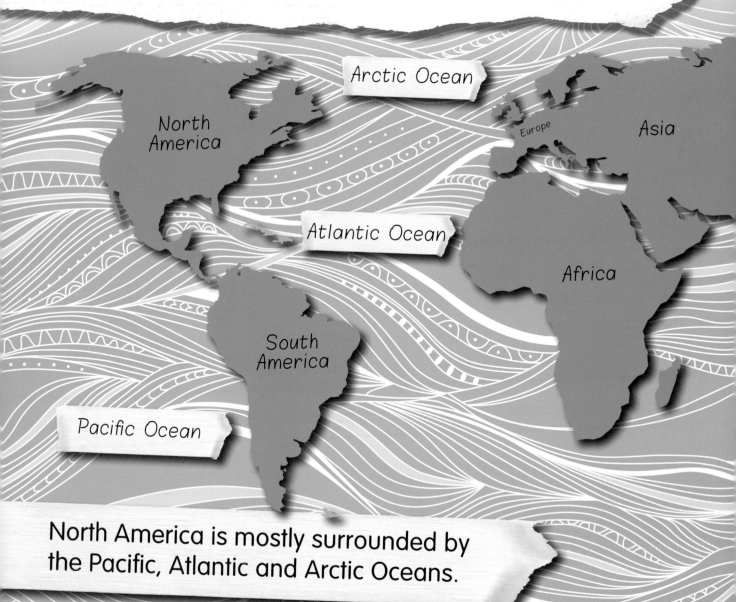

Arctic Ocean

North America

Europe

Asia

Atlantic Ocean

Africa

South America

Pacific Ocean

North America is mostly surrounded by the Pacific, Atlantic and Arctic Oceans.

FACT FILE

Pacific Ocean:
Area: 31% of the Earth's surface
Average Depth: 4,280 metres

Atlantic Ocean:
Area: 15% of Earth's surface
Average Depth: 3,339 metres

Arctic Ocean:
Area: 2.8% of the Earth's surface
Average Depth: 1,038 metres

Depth is how deep the water is.

Arctic Ocean

Atlantic Ocean

Pacific Ocean

COUNTRIES

There are 23 countries in North America. The three largest countries on the continent are the United States of America (U.S.A.), Canada and Mexico.

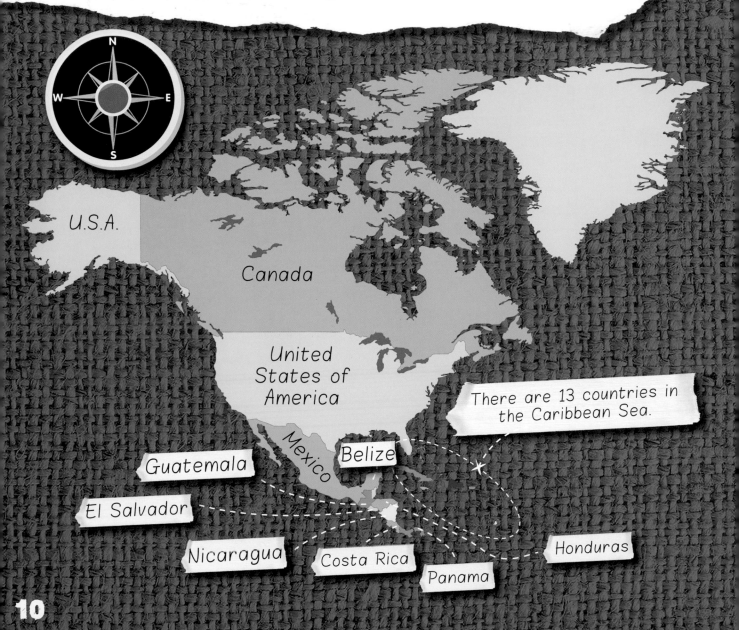

U.S.A.

Canada

United States of America

Mexico

Belize

Guatemala

El Salvador

Nicaragua

Costa Rica

Panama

Honduras

There are 13 countries in the Caribbean Sea.

FACT FILE

Largest Country	Canada	Second largest country in the world
Most Populated Country	United States of America	Over 325 million
Famous Landmark	Statue of Liberty, (U.S.A.)	93 metres high
Highest Peak	Denali, (U.S.A.)	6,190 metres high
Largest Mammal	American Bison	2 metres tall

WEATHER

The North American **climate** changes from the north to the south of the continent. Northern areas of land, such as Greenland and northern Canada, are very cold and are often covered in ice. In winter, temperatures can fall below -20°C.

Polar Bears

Northern Canada

The southern parts of North America, which are located closer to the **Equator**, have a **tropical climate**. The Equator runs along the middle of the planet, which is the warmest part of the world.

Colder

Hotter

Equator

Hotter

Colder

LANDSCAPE

There are many different types of landscape across North America. There are deserts, **grasslands**, lakes, forests and mountains.

Mojave Desert

Grassland

Lake Superior

Tongass National Forest

Rocky Mountains

The largest **mountain range** in North America is called the Rocky Mountains. It stretches along the western side of the continent from Alaska to Mexico.

The Arctic Ocean has extremely cold temperatures because this part of earth faces away from the warm sun. The cold climate freezes the surface of the water and turns it to ice. This is called a **polar ice cap**.

There are many islands in the Caribbean Sea. These islands can have high **mountainous** landscapes, while others can be very small or flat. Many of these are considered to be part of the North American continent.

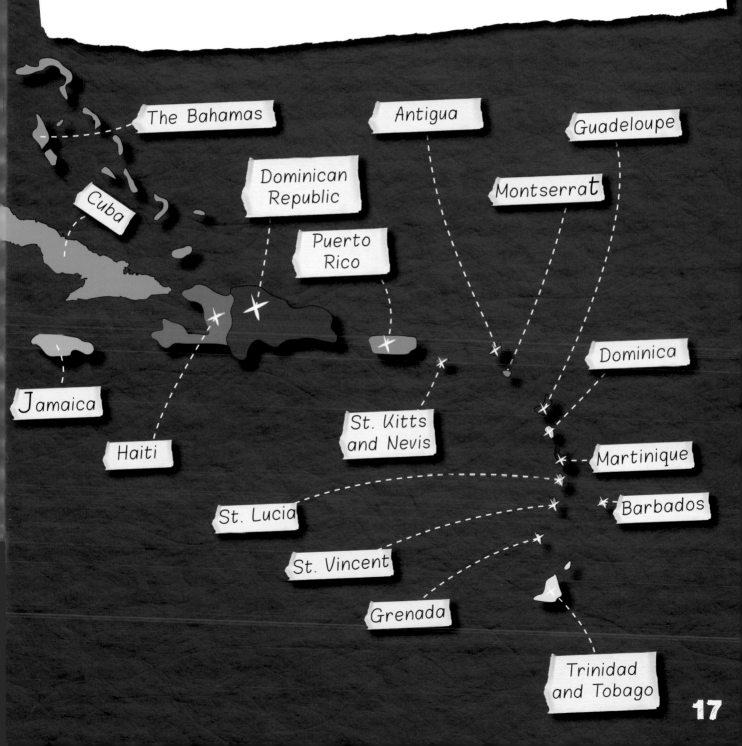

The Bahamas

Antigua

Guadeloupe

Cuba

Dominican Republic

Montserrat

Puerto Rico

Dominica

Jamaica

St. Kitts and Nevis

Haiti

Martinique

St. Lucia

Barbados

St. Vincent

Grenada

Trinidad and Tobago

WILDLIFE

North America is home to many different types of wildlife. It can be found all over the continent.

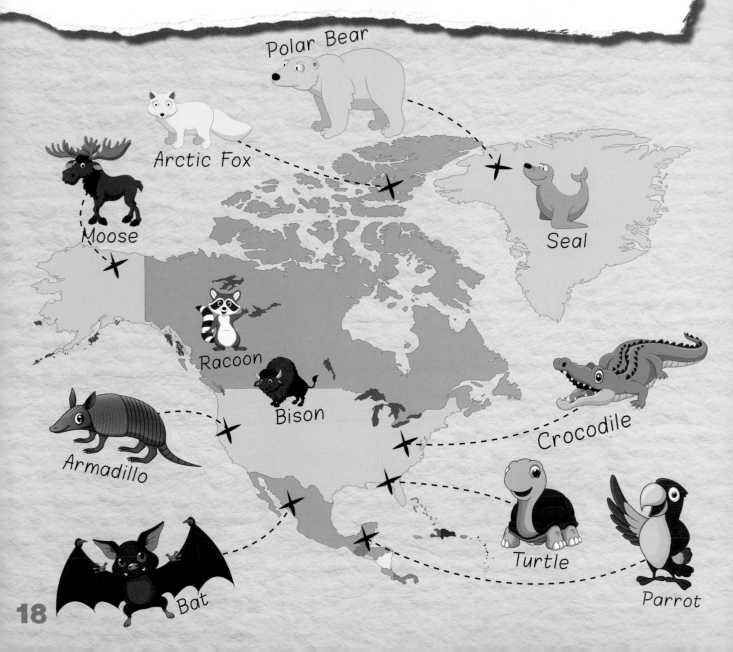

Polar Bear

Arctic Fox

Moose

Seal

Racoon

Bison

Crocodile

Armadillo

Turtle

Parrot

Bat

Polar bears live in the most northern parts of the world. They have thick fur and a layer of fat called blubber to keep them warm in the coldest weather.

Up to 3 Metres

Polar bears can reach over 3 metres when they stand on their back legs.

SETTLEMENTS

Most people who live in North America live in the U.S.A.
The U.S.A. is separated into 50 areas called states.

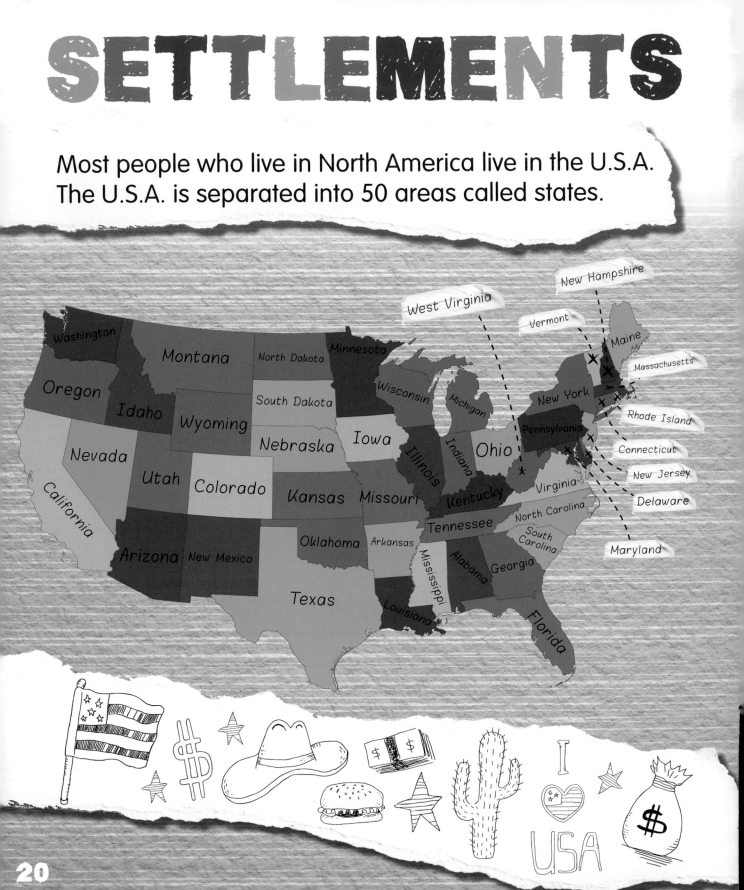

There are many large cities across the continent that have large populations. Mexico City has the highest population at over 22.5 million. Other large cities in North America include New York City, Los Angeles and Toronto.

Mexico City, Mexico

Toronto, Canada

New York City, U.S.A.

Los Angeles, U.S.A.

THE ENVIRONMENT

Many animals in North America are endangered. This means that type of animal is close to becoming **extinct**. To help these animals, special areas of land have been made safe for the animals to live in and be protected. These areas are called conservation parks.

Yellowstone National Park, U.S.A.

GLOSSARY

climate the average weather of an area

Equator imaginary line running around the middle of the earth

extinct a type of animal that is no longer living

grasslands large, flat areas of grassy land

located where something can be found

mammal an animal that has warm blood, a backbone and usually has fur

mountain range a group of connected mountains

mountainous an area of land that has many mountains

polar ice cap sheets of ice that cover the most northern and most southern parts of the world

population number of people living in a place

tropical climate wet and warm weather

INDEX

PHOTOCREDITS

Abbreviations: l–left, r–right, b–bottom, t–top, c–centre, m–middle.

Front Cover Vectors – elenabsl. Front Cover Background – kirillov alexey. Front Coverm – Sanchai Kumar. 2t – IM_photo. 2tr – autsawin uttisin. 2b – Stuart Monk. 3tr – Yongyut Kumsri. 3br – loneroc. 4tl – elenabsl. 5tl – Chris Parypa Photography. 5m – Adam Van Spronsen. 5tr – Orhan Cam. 5bl – f11photo. 5br – loneroc. 6lm – holbox. 7lm – Yongyut Kumsri. 8 – Maria_Galybina. 9m– 89studio, 9 background – taviphoto. 9br – ana_sky. 10 background – kirillov alexey. 11 background – schab. 11m – PILart. 11tr – Artgraphixel. 11br– palasha. 12lm – outdoorsman. 12br – Robyn Mackenzie. 12 background – Yoko Design. 13 background – schab. 13 tape – Picsfive. 14tl – Tupungato. 14tm – turtix. 14tr – Elena Elisseeva. 14bl –Lee Prince. 14br – robert cicchetti. 14 background – GlebStock. 15 background – GlebStock. 15t – Alix Kreil. 15br – Protasov AN. 16ml – Volodymyr Goinyk. 16mr – Henri Vandelanotte. 16 vectors – Erica Truex. 16 background – seamuss. 16mb – John Wollwerth. 17m – Niyazz. 17 background – Goldenarts. 18bl – Pushkin. 18br – Teguh Mujiono. 18mr – AKIllustration. 18m – Teguh Mujiono. 18tm – Genestro. 18br – Muhammad Desta Laksana. 18rm – Teguh Mujiono. 18lm – Muhammad Desta Laksana. 18 background – schab. 19 background – Lonely. 19lm – outdoorsman. 19mr – gillmar. 19bl – MyImages – Micha. 20b – Orfeev. 20 background KannaA – KannaA. 21tl – Gerardo Borbolla. 21tr – SurangaSL. 21bl – cocozero. 21br – View Apart. 21 background – Vladitto. 22ml – Nagel Photography. 22br – Lorcel. 22 background – Ratikova. Images are courtesy of Shutterstock.com. With thanks to Getty Images, Thinkstock Photo and iStockphoto.